FLIGHT OF

ASHES

WRITTEN BY CRYSTAL SLOAN

Flight of Ashes
by
Crystal Sloan

ISBN: 978-1-64545-002-3

Cover Photography
Brittney Najar
@unclebrittany
www.brittneynajar.com

Book Design
Crystal Sloan

Back Cover Photography
Frankie Benavidez
@frankeeb
Frankib777@yahoo.com

@metacrystical
info@metacrystical.org
metacrystical.org
crystalsloan.org

Halos of fire

Tear drops of glass

Everything is vulnerable

When exposed to pressure —

The pleasure of bringing

Ideologies together

And letting them mix

Fixated on an outcome

Too sore to grasp.

For all those who dream in the night,
who have hope in the dark,
who've contemplated giving up,
and continue on despite
every impulse to quit.
You are not alone.

This one's for you.

FORWARD

Devout efforts that we wish would lend a hand to our destiny. So many nights spent in the darkness, in the blackness, in the unknown intensities. Praying for a spark, a light, an illuminated sign to guide the way through what we can't see. I've known this feeling, been familiar with its cadences and its subtleties. It moves in like a ship at night and you don't notice until dawn. We often wonder how we got here. Nestled so deep in the fear and the uncertainty, we often doubt the purpose of our journey. What do we have to lose once we have lost it all? What does the bottom really feel like when it's not ever a place you can truly reach? It's instead an idea, a concept, a feeling; an experience of falling with no end. So how is it exactly that you can rise from this place and begin to start again? What bonds must break and what breaks must mend? These inquires and more stir in the core of my being constantly.

It comes as a direct experience but also, I worry for others who are going through the same thing. These endless cycles of destruction and rebirth; how we can't stop the flow of it. How we have to get out of our own way, or we'll be pummeled by the force of our subconscious mistakes. Those that we can't put off or prevent;

that we must inevitably surrender to the inner forces whose gravity is stronger than that of the dance of a million suns. We can't look directly into it, but we also, can't look away. Within these pages are insights into confessions too stripped to easily identify. Unrecognizable truths. Words I had no other option but to utter. So many things laid out on the table and for the first time I didn't care how they sounded. I ceased the impulse to govern my inner voice and instead let it yell, and slur and stumble dizzyingly towards the horizon of difficult expressions.

I was not concerned about how these poems would be received intellectually, conceptually or grammatically. I felt the context of a word that might not exist properly, but regardless I kept it. As a little marker, as a keepsake, as a tester of boundaries of a world changing too quickly to keep up with. To find some play in the pain, and to find some creativity to something like language which is all too often taken so forcibly serious. So, if you notice something odd, or off beat, or 'incorrect' know it is intentional and is meant to challenge where your judgment and intuition meet. You'll find a coin has actually 3 sides. The 3rd harder to perceive and even more difficult to land on, but it's there.

So often we get caught up in this image of how we're supposed to live. Following prefabricated lists of what we're supposed to do. Provided very limited, superimposed ways in which we're allowed to feel. Call my crazy, but I just don't think it's working. There is something so deeply primal about who we are and why we're here. But through the fog of Walmart's, school systems, and financial divisions it's something we can't seem to notice anymore or don't know how to pay attention to. But it's there. It's always been there and it's not going away anytime soon. It's that feeling in your nervous system when you look up towards visible stars at night. It's that instinct you detect when you gather with others around the warm glow of fire light. It's the might of looking out to the vastness of the ocean and the weight you detect in your heart that simultaneously becomes weightlessness. It is the knowledge that we are somehow connected and a part of everything we feel we are only merely observing.

We have been so misled when it comes to the awareness of our full potential. Our history has been hidden, we have been detracted by distractions, and we daily consume the propaganda of fear and lies; all the while trying to numb the whispers of our own intelligence. Change has become convoluted, scary, unnatural and irrational but this is not the case. Change is necessary, natural, messy and chaotically unorganized — but there is guidance and intelligence there. Though you may not see it, there is a brilliant structure in the way things shift unexpectedly. There must be patience and faith during the long nights. Like the cocoon to the butterfly. Like the fiery death of a Phoenix to new life. Like a wildfire to new growth. Like the womb to the first look in an infant's eyes. Like a story being told that somehow heals the past. The greatest intelligent design is our capacity to move forward and adapt. To begin again. It's what we're designed for; regeneration.

This book is a reflection and a prayer. It is the sinner and the saint. It is the question, the complaint and the medicine all in one. It is a reminder that it is okay to be hurt, to be confused, to be overwhelmed — but these qualities do not define us and are not our permanent homes. They are portals, invitations and transitions. Nothing is as serious as we take it, as we make it out to be. We must remember the pleasure through all the pain and that it is always okay to express yourself and to live in unconventional ways. For truly, this is the only path forward.

It is unwise to take any other road than your own, to meet any one's conditions other than the ones you hold true, or to follow any path that is already paved. Go where it is overgrown because you must find your own way. There is never any shame in stepping out against the grain. Telling your story so that others may do the same.

And when everything burns down, and you come into the light.

You'll remember the moment, when your ashes took flight.

FLIGHT OF

ASHES

Fools Paradise

Everyone is hooked on something.
Everyone is getting their fix somehow.
Everyone is numbing an urge we all share,
A collective impulse,
A collective addiction,
That we're all coping with
Differently.
We're high on it more than caffeine
It's;
Nostalgia.

Burning Snow

How do I take
The things
That burst me
Into flames
And turn them into
Snowflakes?
How do I make order
Out of the things
That would rather
Remain untamed?
How can heat slow down,
Becoming something less consuming,
And more reflective?
How can we
Cycle the elements
So, we too,
Can become
Regenerative?

Honey Pots and Cedar Trees

The birds and the bees
What a fancy and happy thing
To float among the world
Making honey and singing songs;
Lessons we all could learn from.
How to pollinate things and help their growing,
How to make nests for the things we care for,
So they may receive warmth, comfort and security,
How to fly and not confuse it for falling,
Letting go of our feet so that we may experience
wings.
There is so much to learn,
From the birds and the bees.

By Any Other Name

Rain falls and
Awakens me,
I dreamt of my mother
And intolerable conditions I am fighting to change.
Over and over again,
The same.
Deeper breaths
And gentleness from the Earth,
Healing my wounds
Only by cleaning them first,
I arrive new
Even though I feel defined,
For those illusions
Exist solely in my mind,
Who I really am
Can only be found
In my heart.

LIBERATION INSURGENCY

Perpetual choices,
In or out of alignment –
Open road;
Always the right choice.
Desperate winds seeking
Well kept hair,
Mangling cordial appearances
And prim ambition.
Decisions we are left to make
Only guided by whispers
Of angels,
Creeping through ancient
Canyons and seeping through
Faulted cracks
Beneath the shadow
Of a world that used to be
Sleeping.
Beneath a fixed eclipse;
Moonlight will set you free,
Blinding violent rage;
Masked and naked –
Ordered to tell the truth.
But with language desecrated
We struggle with unchoreographed
Tongues.

We have only begun to remember
How truly vacant
We've been.
Mistaken in our investments,
Gears and steam and currency
In exchange for our sovereignty,
Humbling place to be -
Bitten by the hand that feeds.

Some Like it Hot

I'm afraid to admit,
I'm afraid to write;
I'm scared.
The hope for myself,
The hope for others,
The hope for the world;
That I have - is real.
My feelings are intense.
And I only feel them heightening.
Distraught by my need to be balanced,
But forthright;
To be available, but productive;
To be courteous, but strong;
To be upbeat, but driven;
To be accommodating, but structured;
To be feminine, but real;
To be smart, but unexpected;
To be relevant, but new;
To be worldly, but accessible;
To be interesting, but off-beat;
All of these things pull at me.
But, honestly, I just want
To be loved
Simply for being myself.

Annihilation Ancillary

The things we need to express
Are more prominent now
Then they've ever been.
No time for poor thoughts,
So easily encouraged to.
Dawning diligence shining
Early morning light into the
Night of the soul we're
Breaking through.
It is not me that needs
Needing,
It is not the effect that
Needs causing,
It is our Love that needs
Attending.

Identity Syndicate

Why are poets always looking
For something lost?
Abandonment plagued pasts,
And secretive thought conceptions -
Functioning in a world
Out of flux
With their soul.
Whiskey bottles and the curves
Adorning the bodies of women,
Their answers are found there
No more than they are found
In the soil of the Earth,
Or the terrain on Mars.
Impending destruction of the self,
All the while putting nose to ground
Trying to find it.
Sedative, yet, trying to wake.
Cursed success follows,
And the destructive glorification continues.
I thought these vices must be mine.
I thought I, too, must
Mistreat my youth,
Validate my hurt and
Fuel my pain by the things that
Seemed to take it away.

But that only brought me more.
Isolation; is real,
But self-fulfilling.
I've found the poet's path is
A rhythmatic mirage;
Ghosts and angels walk side by side,
And the demons are never
In plain sight.
But if you're seeking to be found
You will always remain
Lost.
It was when I discovered
I didn't need everything that triggered me
To have insight
Into my own condition.
When I attained the bravery
To look into the mirror
Without whiskey coated eyes,
Or to see into the soul of another
Without a need for them to fill,
It was when the mastery of
My own mind
Overcame the mystery
Of it's dark side
That I found my
Writing more clear.
No one is wounded too extreme
For healing,

No one is lost in a sea of
Interconnectivity,
Decades have been lived in
This lostness.
Shattering clarity;
It's time
To begin again.

Laudable Propensity

I spent the whole morning trying to validate myself.
Wondering if I said too much.
If there was too much feeling.
If there was too much honesty.
Was I just babbling?
Lacking poignant abilities.
Am I flopping or swimming?
I can't tell -
They seem to require the same effort.
So I'm confused, but not really.
I'm nervous, but not really.
I'm unrefined and lineless,
I struggle at times in the interactions
With others.
So delicate is their piece of mind,
And, I, my own.
I shatter when it's not reciprocal.
And I don't know why.
My own skylined expectations sometimes keep
Me from holding any ground at all.
But I dream, but I love - greatly,
Is this not enough?
I grow tired of sheltered thoughts.
Not wanting to impose reflection
To those who are scared of mirrors.

Light blinds us all,
It's just all about the angle.
Can I keep my peace still?
Can I maintain my own heart beat as I
Would well encourage another to do?
Perhaps I know - perhaps I know what
You are going through better than you do.
I hope my deeper intention is revealed;
That a fulfilling life should be more than
A luxury,
A rarity,
A reservation;
It's the greatest birthright
Granted to us all.

CEREBRAL HOSTILITIES

History in the making;
That's your life.
I'm home always.
Departure; what an interesting concept.
Arrival; preceding the thought.
It's a battle, not of blood,
But of understanding.
Right now we're at war with
Our beliefs.
Beaten and disoriented
Only the brave are standing.
Caught in the crossfire,
Heavy hearts lead the way.
Dragging; limbs, friends and denial.
All of them resisting
Just the same.

FUTILE HYPOCRISY

Uncanny;
Union and disarray.
Brilliant temples of thought pave our past -
The ringing of their absence
Sounds the way.
The fondness and the wandering,
Pretty much all the same.
Buried.
Married.
We push with the force
Of one hundred bulls.
And we create damage just the same
Where are the thoughts of silk?
Where is the fine texture of our hemmed respects?
The gentleness;
Armor of compassion
And battles full of empathy.
Yes, we may disagree;
But it's not worth dying for -
Never is,
Never has,
Never will be.
Truth just as perverted as our sanity;
Sold short on golden years
And youthful campaigns of the heart.

Stiff faces and shifty eyes preoccupy
Most of those working hard to work harder,
Unsettled bones and fuming blood,
They descend just the same.
It was never part of the plan.
Of course not, what is?
Withholding the assumptions of particular
dispositions
We weren't intended to build barriers between
each other,
Life is meant for bridges and waterfalls.

Apocryphal Flings

No one seems to have great love around me
Deprived of true affection, we settle
For the closest version of normality.
But nothing is 'normal'.
Different things work for different
People.
It's what 'works'.
People have different needs.
Great love exists in many places,
In-between where we think it should be.
All people are deserving of love
And affection.
This goes without contest.
But, where is the romance?
Where is the belief and devotion in
True partnership?
Where does it lie and how do you
Celebrate its priorities?
When your heart beat falls,
It's a cue that something's out of place.
If it's flying, well,
That's a whole other case.
I believe in great love still,
Even though all I see is dissatisfaction.
We've turned into chronic liars.

Regardless of our intention.
We best lie to ourselves.
If we believe this lie
Then it becomes truth
To everyone else.
The mind is very convincing,
The ego is very misleading,
And the soul is very quiet.
It actually won't even bother the other two
While they duke it out.
Head-butting, like male rams in a
Territorial dispute.
The soul will stand still.
Silent in disengagement.
Unattended and dormantly opinionated.
Until the pace is switched.
Until the argument subsides.
Until there is harmony that lullabies
The chaos,
The purpose of life itself will not be
As clear.
The simpleness; undiscovered.
Change; impossible without the inability
To process.
Working gears, but no machine.
We find ourselves entrusting our fate
To well and sensible things,
Forgetting reality is an illusion anyways.

Umbilical Turmoil

Sequential beliefs that tether us
That bind us
That lead us down paths of remembrance
Who are we to cut cords from our ancestry?
Forgetting appropriateness of divine sensations;
Re-establishing the trust between states of life and
birth;
The female calling.
The truth of her blood, and her screams, and her
laugh;
All of which have the power to heal or condemn.
So does that not mean that she can then
Burn or bless it all?
Does it not mean that the hand of a woman propels
All other things?
In the seeing of our original chaos, why is it so
Confusing
To understand our basic need;
To rise back into our motherly understanding,
Gathering sisters and whispers of a world
Corrected and resurrected,
Bandaged, kissed and mended –
Astoundingly possessed by love,
The origination of our souls.
The ending and beginning to it all.

Getting Out of Your Own Way

I had such a beautiful morning.
I rose before the sunlight,
Turns out I've been oversleeping.
Who knew such a thing
Could be so violent
To the body.
Depressive, heavy and tense,
I thought I was going crazy;
Turns out I needed to get my ass out of bed.
I'm definitely ready for some permanent healing.
Transitioning into and out of a life more in sync
and aligned
With my inner purpose and deepest expression.
I can no longer hide or play sheep or sheep herder
I am neither, and I am coming out
Forthright with my
Destiny.
We are all made for great things,
It's just allowing them to happen.

ROMANTICS OF THE MOON

Why is my heart awaiting your arrival?
Short stops and long roads,
It's a game of endurance.
Wise choices and witty replies;
We feel restless when we're misunderstood.
Traveling by thought or by feet
To the places we feel held,
And attended to.
Where the negotiations of our needs
Become more clear,
And we can move into
Ourselves a little bit more.
Because the point in life
Is to be truthful
And we so often
Hold our tongues
For much more than special occasions,
And it becomes numbing.
Everything feels the same,
And colors take on a duller shade
Without the light of passionate play.
Romantics of the moon,
Unite again in our honest illuminations -
And carry the dawn fiercely.
We were meant for wild relationships with nature,

Speaking languages of only timing,
All words fly away and leave you with a feeling;
Heartwarming and smooth to the belly.
Our courage builds our foundation for
compassionate living,
For calm living,
For awakened living,
For vitality,
And the belief of abundance.
Practices of gratitude
Turn water into wine,
And wine into water.
I couldn't always say
I was this ready,
I'm just so used to things falling away.
So I might as well set sail -
I just hope,
You catch
My drift.

Hold on Loosely, But Don't Let Go

To look through eyes
Drifting softly in seas
Of eradicating dreams,
Challenged amidst our own denial
And accepting of things
Which shouldn't be valued as such.
We lose and gain in the same time frame,
And we chase the tail
Of things we'll never become;
Things we would never want
If we knew the cost.
There's elements,
They're the elephants in the room.
How to use them?
When tools are broken and information burned
And our fate is in the hands of those
Who know nothing but to grip.
Suffocating caresses.
They've made a mess of our villages,
Hungry and hunting and finding nothing.
Mother nature; always so providing;
Has a might that still hurts,
A might that stings and burns
And rips to shreds those things that are comforting
Of our Earthly experience.

With One Willing Encounter

There is nothing you can not show me,
Nothing I feel called to turn away from,
Your deepest truths or your most buried
Secrets;
I am now ready.
Show the beauty of the Earth to me in it's most
rural spaces,
Show me your slaughterhouses and your industries
of death,
Show me the intelligence of bees choosing to seek
out a flower,
And show the carcasses of your shipping methods
strewn along the
Beach of Chittagong,
Show me everything, because all of it is true.
I can no longer hide from being uncomfortable -
It pervades my existence anyways.
Domestication hasn't tamed me yet;
Wild is a super power.
It means we can survive anything.
So why do we not rely on this enduring quality
more?
Our ability to cope and to change is miraculous,
We just have to want to breathe breath into it.
Give it our attention,

And accept that our hands have been wet with
blood;
And they too, can run clean in the river.
I see our delicate ironies and the soft joy of a life
lightly lived,
And we are granted the right to live in every way;
As long as it does not compromise the welfare of
others.
I go into the jungle and I remember everything.
But it starts to become unclear when I return back
to the city.
How do we bridge who we think we are
With who were supposed to be?
I am strong and wise and have learned
To carry burdens to the places they need to go,
And to lay them down there;
To create ceremony for their departure.
To burn them and to dream anew.
We have forgotten this cyclical co-creative force
That used to govern our societies
Long before religion and economies.
Asking permission of the plants
And singing songs to the rising sun,
This was life before industry had begun.
But the fascination people have for manufactured
life
Is too seductive for them to see the truth of our
history.

So instead you will just be labeled;
A hippie, a tree hugger or any other slandered
name that mocks and deviates
Having a genuine connection
To the Earth and your own body.
See, we are living in a sea of probabilities and
mystical happenings
But society seems to have turned it's cheek
And has found more interest in the endless pursuit
of things.
Concurring that this is a valuable way of living.
But this way of living
Only works
If you see reality as separate.
Our greatest challenge is that I don't experience
what you do
And that my fate is assumed to rest
Is the nest of a separate womb than yours.
We have the same Mother Earth,
And the same Father Sky,
And we have the same responsibility to open up all
the blinds,
To see what has been happening as we chose to
turn a blind eye,
Why are we kicking and screaming when it comes
to seeing ourselves?
With one willing encounter, the healing
commences.

In The Dark

Set your whispers to fire, angel.
Set your secrets ablaze with ferocity
And watch your gentleness simmer and boil
Into the strength that can summon the seas.
Into air that breathes the world into being
And deep into roots for the gestation
Of our due nourishment.
Into the thriving of
A future yet to come;
One that pioneers peace.
The only one we have
Been relentlessly
And incessantly
Dreaming of.

Assertive Assumptions

Courage is just a word until you feel it's breath
Upon the nape of your neck.
Standing hairs and the feeling of a presence;
You're not alone in these moments
   -   and you know it.
Our prayers are simply calls upon those
Who are already listening;
So they respond pretty quickly.
Because space and time is a mystery.
And we've lost interest in our imaginations,
So the imagery is hard to invent on your own.
Surely our stories are all we've ever had,
But now we have books teaching outdated truths
And assertive assumptions
We really don't have the answers to.

Falconer

The hardest thing for me to admit,
Is that I need no one else,
And everyone -
All at the same time.
It's our relating that has me wondering,
What is mine and what is yours?
And what difference does it make if the point
In life
Is not to focus on our diversity?
We build and chip
At the architecture of things,
When really we would be better
Becoming the tailors of wings.

Legions of the Lioness

All the women I have let down,
All the women I didn't believe had my back,
All the ways I abandoned my own needs,
I am here to resuscitate
The collective lungs we all share.
To admit my faults and heal my scars,
I am present now with open and loving arms.
You see, I never thought
The answer lied within my capacity
To forgive.
I looked down, looked up, looked away
And negated the only path for revival;
The one within.
Now, I take my stride,
I hold my own hand proudly and I bring my eyes
Upon my own body
And I feel a dearness
That was once rejection.
I choose to heal that false misperception,
And turn it back into truth.
Back into gold,
And flowers and drips of jasmine.
Honey and bee stings and the protection of
ourselves.
For if we do not choose

To roar;
To bite;
To claw;
We will perish
While the dishonored preachers prey on the
sleeping.
Rest, my dear,
Do not deny yourself that necessity,
But know when it is time to rise;
For oversleeping we now
Have no luxury for.
Remember; our calls
And groans are meant
To awaken
The others
Who've fallen too deeply asleep
In their unconscious slumber.

Puppet Strings and Dinner Dates

Silent and simple,
Lust aside -
We are strong.
Stronger than puppets
Held by heavy weight finishing lines;
Ready to break.
Though we make dinner dates
Of ourselves anyways.
How can we cultivate more consideration
Without losing our sanity?
Bullet proof jackets and rusty armor,
We're consumed within the protection of honor
And have little interest in that which may
Be festering underneath.
Freedom is a thought.
The action is much different.
We hold the key to it all.
In a world of production is repetition and insanity
Paralleling lines of existence?
And is it our thoughts that cross it?
Or our feeling?
And in which way
Are we truly limited?
I take blows and fires and falls
And I inject space into those places

That seem overwhelmed
And calmness comes too,
Through the delicate belief in it.
Creative tailors whether we desire the role or not,
Impaled by the same weapon designed to cut new
paths,
We feel the urge to throw ourselves upon sharp
things
Considering it selfless and necessary,
But we don't seem to have the tools for cauterizing.
And do we let too much out or too little in?
Beginning and ending in the same conversations
We need renewal more than it needs us,
Because it's a force of its own intended to play out
Regardless,
So our relaxation is the exact thing
We need the most.
Some call it surrender; others - processing,
Assimilating, forgiving,
But it's the same -
All of it.
Put plainly;
Let's call it
Acceptance.

What Makes Me Weak

You said you missed me
But I don't know what that means,
It's hard for me to connect
With the feeling of missing something
I don't interpret as mine.
That I can't possess.
That simply passes in
My waiting.
Shape shifting in the
Blink of an eye,
Becoming something
I can't recognize,
I hardly hold my breath;
For what I can't control.
And yet I as well
Am at the whim of it all.
It is the smoothness of
Fluid things that is alluring,
Shining and calming,
But they also have a tendency
To crash without warning.
They assume and swell
Whether or not
We've embraced ourselves,
And they perform in harmony

With gravities of conduction.
You say you miss me
But of what force is it you are speaking?
Is it the realm of my body?
Is it the eagerness of my heart?
Is it the hint of a person
I bring forth
Upon meeting my obligations?
Are you proud?
I don't miss often,
And I don't miss missing people,
But when I do;
It usually takes me out
At the knees.

The Bigger Picture

Where do we go with our pain?
Having to admit so much but not a confessional in
sight.
We experience so much solely;
And I suppose we always have.
Aspects of our own making
What will it take to admit we aren't in control of it
all?
Where is our embracing, our holding?
When hugging has become something
controversial?
How do we then become our own sanctuary?
Nature speaks quiet promises that we've forgotten
how to trust.
All I need is a soothing voice now,
But so many angry and fed up tones
Dispel from the rigid mouths
Of everyone suffering from
The same afflictions.
So when the desire is to no longer wallow
Where are the congregations that lack despair?
The celebration of life outside of baby showers,
weddings,
And promotions at work.
I'm seeking rewards of the heart and

Inspiration to the imagination;
But only finding time for mundane tasks.
I came home today wanting to be held
But I found only my dogs inflicted with their own
turbulence,
From my absence and the commitments I've made
To make ends meet.
And this unrest at times can seem more magnified
By the tedious balance of caring for ourselves
While lending a gracious hand
To everyone else.
When will we become aware
That the quality of life
Lies within the quality of our service
To the greater whole.

APPROPRIATE ARRIVALS

How often I forget how easy it is
For miscommunication to ensue,
To burrow and nestle into the depths
Of even our most honest endeavors.
To unearth and rebirth forgotten tendencies
We wished to lay to rest.
Haunting shadows of repeated behavior.
When can we undo the burials
We've endured?
Resurrected;
Can we be forgiven?
Can it be forgotten?
When does satiable memory
Become a guiding lighthouse
For the turbulence of this world?
The mighty beacon of hope,
Where is it to be found?
Is the light in the sky
Ours to create?
Or is the light of the moon enough?
Is it then the tide?
Is it then the sea?
Is it then the pull and tug of these things
We can't quite perceive
Welling up from the deepest depths of us?

The things we feel
Must be true,
But we can't always identify
Why they surface when they do.
Triggers.
Chiggers to the spirit.
Uncomfortable admissions.
We're always led to places we must correct.

Fettle Grind

Surgical center;
11:01 am
Fox tails whispering in the wind
From the outside patio.
2 hours in counting,
And the city's alive.
So is the medical industry.
We file in like produce from a stand,
Market tags and skews,
Barcoded names and number games,
Each five minutes somebody new.
They pour in like a conference
Of businessmen, but they've come
To be healed.
The irony of our emotional
Stances.
How to complain about western medicine
When they caught my mother's cancer early?
Pretty fountains, orchid flowers
And glass stairways;
Presentation or comfort?
Does it even matter when you
Get four bills from 3 people?
Charged for different times
Of the day.

Be happy we 'saved you'.
Glad I followed through with my job
With all that time lost
These benefits are really paying off.
I'm so grateful and nauseous
All at the same time.

WOMAN

Woman;
Child of the Earth.
Bearers of starlight
And birthers of a life whose origins
We have yet to pin point.
Dreamers of heavy news
And caressers of the dismantled,
Healers of the shamed
And translators of the wind.
Confined by the sins of society,
We now awaken to a greater simplicity,
The one they abandoned in the backwoods
Of their preaching.
Power is not authority.
Power is grace and understanding.
An ability to see Love
At the root of all things.
Woman who holds the bell
That dispels all mistruth;
Be vigilant in your ringing.
Pasts of silence,
It's now too loud to remember how it was
When it was more quiet.
She should awaken with the dawn
Like she always has,

And let the sunshine fall
So deeply into her skin,
That is seeps into her heart
And reflects out
Regardless
Of where she goes.

Desperate Caresses

Can it be told what becomes of those
Who dream endlessly,
Who wait for the materialization
Of the immaterial.
Frightening, elating, new;
Lonely day dreams worlds away,
The feeling that it is right under your nose anyway.
The frustration in seeing and believing but not
touching.
How touch deprived we are,
How we need it
How we crave it;
Still we refuse to reach,
To extend; to offer.
Cursed gestures and convoluted displays
Of what we
Call affection.
Sad, twisted little offerings.

Entwined Contradictions

Expecting people to be
Responsible for your emotions
Is like waking up
And holding someone responsible
For your dreams;
They're your own.

I'm sick of fighting people,
For themselves.
Love.
It's like someone put a manual for a
Hundred gallon saltwater aquarium
Into the assembly box
Of a fucking wooden rocking chair.

We're often worlds away
Even when we're standing
Eye to eye.
And I don't always think
This is such a bad thing.
We have endless room to create
And yet we ache and creek in
The absence of validation
For what is our own to occupy.

I have to think life is a constant

Process -
Of rusting what has become
Unattended.
Technical errors
Happen without merit,
And we pay the ultimate cost
For the lack of our awareness,
And the willingness to disregard
What we don't yet fully understand.

Human Windows

Showing face
Showing up
Not the same things.
Clear eyes
Shining eyes
Far away eyes;
They show the truth.
The action of our conviction
Comes forth through our
Perception;
And it shows in our eyes,
Clouded, clear, invisible,
Seen
Or in-between what we are
Experiencing;
Unknown.
Mirrored by other souls.
What do you see?
A fluctuating world constantly
Recreating itself
Can be made new
By a single glance.

Desert Hearts

Impatience -
What an encourager;
How revealing
Of our weak and tender wounds.
Powerful -
Awakening to what spites us;
Tweezer to the splinter
That dug in when
We touched the world.
Absurd aftermath of our birth,
Helpful and haunting,
Sharp and microscopic,
Frustration that bends us
To rest more compassionately
Into the understanding of
Each other.
Seas of cactus brush;
Watch your step,
Prickly roads ahead,
Blushed,
Red,
Adorned,
Caught in the corners of time.

MERCY'S GATE

Vanity is being
Gentle coddled
By the ripe hands
Of fear,
Catalyst for greed,
Blindingly denied,
Self-impairing;
Community desecrator.
You take nothing with you
But the love you create,
The love you share,
The capacity you have
To hold space
For your own
Self-understanding.

Dear New Years

Dear New Years,
How easy it is to forcefully shove your glittery
And optimistic self
Into the tight and meaningless
compartmentalization
All the other commercial holidays occupy.
Renewal; yes, what a concept.
Reflection; intention,
Necessary for the sustainability of growth.
Crowds of people gather, strangers; misled.
What makes it different than any other fucking
day?
Because people claim it to be some sort of high
value.
Somehow important to have a loving face next to
yours
That you can reach to and touch lips.
Now's the time to have a plan and
Now's the time to set it in motion.
Let it all go. Drop it with the ball.
Start over. Forget yesterday.
Dismiss your sins for there is truly no sinning.
New Years; you have the same standard as beauty.
Illusive and without true form

Simply molding to our own idea and injected
purpose.
Where the meaning carries no weight.
Only serving the burden of comparison and the
Toxic buildup of artificial happiness.
Dressed in dazzling adornments
We selfishly shield ourselves
From the harm of our current lifestyles.
We must learn to forgive,
But the forgetting seems a bit too premature.
Forgetting is the naivety of a selfish culture
Seeking acknowledgement
In all the outlandishly wrong places.
How can it be that we attempt to meet standards
We didn't collectively create?
Tell me something real. I grow tired of dreams. Of
longing.
Dressing up dreary wishes in order to make it
Through my day, through my life.
I have little patience for anything less than
greatness
And why do I feel so shy to enforce that?
Why do I feel so nervous to live in truth?
Because it always separated me from the crowd
Even more than already happens naturally.
We all know what we need to do. Don't we?
Couldn't we figure it out, change, re-create
anything

At the welling up of the feeling itself?
Riding the impulse of change
With the action it takes
To bring about 'fresh' things.
It can't just be New Years Eve.
It's not about figuring it out in a single heartbeat.
It's enjoying the ride and facilitating the changes
constantly.
Limited beliefs were offered with no cost.
We've been taught to be excited about
What comes free.
Sheltered in our own mindsets,
It will always be only shadows on the wall
Until we confront the fear
That comes with fire.

Dove Medicine

Dove medicine.
Unorthodox angels making themselves known
Cooing in change
Smooth as milk to a babe,
Nourishing to the self just the same.
I drink from silver
And give thanks to clay,
To dirt and bone and the formations of our bodies.
We are the original home.
Marrow of stars and keeper of the ground.
Feathered spirits have always
Invited us to soar,
Through visitation and song
We have always been looked after.
And always inspired to dream of new heights.
We tussle with turmoil
And have always looked to the sky
To settle our fears.
Aloneness is absent in presence,
But is also the only experience found.
Into the emersion of it all –
We find ourselves
Again and again.
Like a quiet walk;
We are renewed each time we find a deeper truth

Conscious and willing,
We can always regenerate
Tired wings.

MAD HATTER

What if you write a book
And it gets lost forever,
Would you get lost?
I heard of a man,
Saw him with my own eyes.
He lost 13 novels.
In an instant.
Just like that.
He seemed pretty okay,
But with a hostile calm.
Perhaps we are all
Always a blink away
From total and complete
Madness.

Deciphering Ambiguity

1245 16th street.
Santa Monica, CA;
Alkaline bodies,
Acidic bodies,
Blend in the streets.
We're told how to live and
We're told how to die,
And both seem just as interesting.
How often we live life in a
Figurative way.
Are the conversations I have with myself
Revealing or persuading?
Are they the same thing?
I get lost in my own hypothetical situations.
There is no singular way to live and be.
Though it seems pretty clear it should include;
Kindness.
How often we take advantage
Of simplicity.
So many paths, so many twists
And turns but the point is to
Keep driving.
The ocean seems to know something
We've forgotten.
Deep breaths full of salt air

And the heaviness fades.
All it takes is one sunset
To wash it all away.
Nothing to birth,
Nothing to bury.
At ease with the living.
Shores of sunshine flood
My darkest doubts.
They still like to make themselves
Known from the shadows,
But as I told a friend yesterday,
We must carry the torch still.

Simple Truths

Destiny does not
Just exist in the
Physical world.
It exists in memory,
In thought,
In feeling,
In a word.
Sometimes it's what we don't do
That defines us.
The weight of the world we
Convincingly cling to,
Is ours to
Choose.
Delicate or mountainous,
Delightful or depleting,
Apathetic or inspiring,
We're paving the way now;
For who we will become.
Advancements of a different kind.
We're receiving gentle reminders,
As the weight we experience.
The relationship we have
With the things around us.
People, events, environments.

They're showing the way
By the deep hurt of our
Triggering.
Who and what provokes us there?
That is what needs evaluating.
Our healing is in recalibrating.
The responsibility we have put
On others to care for
Aspects that we should be
Caring for ourselves.
It's time to take back
The power we gave away thinking
It was someone else's.
No matter what it appears to be
Whether someone hurt you,
Or built you up only to walk away,
Or whether it puts strain
On those who cannot and will never
Be able to bear your pain -
We must get back to what's important.
We must mend our bold negligence
With simple truths.

Dwindling Prospects

I've come to realize
I am still a very well programmed American.
I came to the conclusion from listening to a jazz
song.
I have my clothes I get to pick and choose,
Some I've never worn,
But just in case the occasion arrived.
I have a printer
And a phone
And a carnival of necklaces;
Things
Things
Things,
But I don't have
One thing that most Americans
Don't have...
And that's touch.
Healthy affection,
Laughter and dog piles
Of loving bodies.
It's probably why people think I'm flirtatious,
It's probably why I reach out to touch everyone I
meet,
Time is short, it's passing;
And so are we...

Why not share in the company?
I return home alone.
It's quiet and sweet.
Most times.
But it's lonely.
I've started to pour tea for myself
In the evenings
Instead of wine.
I hope it will last.
I'm listening to my body, I guess.
Word's on the street that most things we do
Aren't very healthy,
And still we continue to play out our programming;
TV, cigarettes, scotch and smoothies,
Shopping, collecting, counting and shipping,
Trailers of agony, I think –
Maybe I'm wrong,
But I do feel alone at times in this
Uh... Awakening? Remembering? Becoming?
Realizing? Vision? Precision? Paying attention?
Hallucination? Self-fulfilling creation? Destiny?
Anarchy? Transferring to a higher state of
conscious living?
I have many theories.
They keep me pretty busy.
But most days, these days,
I just want to drop them all.

Green Shoots and Starlight

Illuminated nights,
Telling of the winds direction and force
By it's field,
By it's feel.
Spectacular advancements
Projecting us into dreams and
New beginnings,
Realms of majestic intensities
Belonging and becoming;
Always.
And at it's very root
We too have origins similar,
To the brilliance of seeds -
Sprouting and reaching towards
Sunshine;
And all that is divine.

Harmonic Revival

Even the birds seem stressed here.
Their chirps are not quite as playful,
Their calls; more seeking.
Their patterns, more at the whim of the patterns of
our own.
Our driving, our building, our noises and our
proliferations -
Invasive to the joyful moments in between
Foraging for food and endless pursuits of survival.
We can experience more of who we are.
Deep moments of relaxation exchanged for a life
That seems to be scurrying past us
And we have chosen
To stay busy instead.
Clouds move only at the pace of the wind.
We've become ships in the night,
And we have no idea how truly close we are.
Continuing through hard times
We haven't been left with many options.
I quit the blame game the second I ran out of
fingers.
I'm not here to create another failed story line,
Or to try to manage anyone else's timelines but my
own.

I like sitting still and quiet, and I find much solace
in it.
I like my body and our conversations together.
I prefer intuition over plans most days.
I remember that we used to live in cyclical ways,
And some still do this.
Our beginning starts with bare feet on naked Earth;
Concrete blocks -
Let's grab our jack hammers and unlock them.
It's time to abandon our pitchforks and
Find some more useful tools,
Cause there is so much work here to do.
Chastised purities and awkward legislation,
The devil sleeps in our immature agreements.
Broken down by my own pride,
I have no more luxury of a place to hide;
I too have been singing a sad song
That I do not really wish to hear again.
I want to bring back songs of strong hearts
And generational endurances,
Keepers of the gardens of our ancient past
And our forgotten heritage.
How are we always where we're supposed to be?
We can learn to herd our thoughts to the right
pastures.
I find more movement in stillness than stillness in
Movement these days;
But both exist.

And are encouraged by the shepherd of our hearts.
This is the war zone;
Not the paradise.
Paradise is the responsibility of living in harmony,
The celebration of free time and space to be,
The abundance that comes from living in union
with water.
There are subtle aspects that paint the picture
Of the human condition
And what it means to experience it.
I'm learning to comfortably live inside myself.
To know what I can and cannot change,
And accept the way I choose to show up;
For myself.
How I hold space
For my own resurgence
Is the preface
To my full resurrection.

Otherwise, Boundless

Now how do you recall the classic understanding,
The nuance in our active imaginings,
Portrayed and gestured by our peers,
The likely and cunning
Candidates of our memories.
Song and dance romance our purpose,
That filling with life;
The effort that is worth living.
Recalled delusions where
We chose not to get along.
Forward notions; we belong among the future.
Too starry-eyed for tall tales
And too revered for quiet progress,
We dream aloud and cultivate desire
As we attempt to drive the life we live
With the undocumented version
Of who we can become.

Temperament Toning

How can I focus on other things?
Children waiting for gustation
A womb full of wisdom
And I feel empty.
Is it the writer's symptom
Or desolation in the path of illusive love?
I work on my own pleasures
And aim to aid those in their own seeking,
Yet I've truly to find someone who feels my craving
In their fingertips.
And it makes me wonder
If it exists,
Though I've experienced it before.
Undoubtedly it exists tangibly in the moments
I find between the sun rise
And it's slumber.
Where are the people who value heartbeats and
breathing?
I'll tell you they are everywhere, but perhaps...
Just scared.
And I've been working so diligently
On abandoning all my fear,
But I'm wondering
If it's presence is like suffering
And, if it too, is not intended to go away;

Though I pray constantly for it's dissipation.
Perhaps today was heavy for a reason
As I returned to a compromising job to pay my bills,
And learned of those doing the same
That became absent in their writing,
Who had a cancerous kidney removed,
And another; a heart attack.
And perhaps I'm just feeling the residuals of that.
Coming in contact with familiar pain.
Holding space for each other
Isn't easy.
But kindness is.
And that's what I exercise.
But perhaps it's myself,
That needs the most repetitions.

Four Foot Fire Lanes

We went separate ways, but never parted.
I told you to abandon your efforts,
The ones long gone from the brush of my skin.
The ones you attempted in mind and faulted
friendship.
The ones I wanted more of –
Those of the heart;
Were the ones that weren't available,
Yet, were so vastly undeniable.
And you admitted everything,
But still had tied hands and sadness
At your limited expression.
How often we long for a way to become more
Known to ourselves,
And, to another.
How frequent the quest of belonging
Strays us from familiar terrain.
Why must we shun from hardship
And why must we glorify the seemingly easy?
Because that, too, contains unknowns and
struggles and risks.
Too denied to remember that life is never free
Of consequence.
This too, must be recalled and reinforced;
That escape routes

We're never intended to be used as plans
Or exit strategies,
They're for when shit's on fire
And you need to get the fuck out.
They were put in place for emergencies only;
Not to be used
To get a little fresh air.

Thompson Fire

The hills are burning
Visions injected with sporadic
Palpitations of orange and red flames
Pouring into areas
Where people have lived and thrived
Fought and loved and developed character.
In houses and parks and street corners
Where people were students and teachers and
friends
And lovers;
Pathways paved for destinies unraveling,
In the midst of living life itself;
It's hard when it stops.
The pause similar that happens to the breath -
The inhale, the exhale and the fluctuation of depth,
The emergence of something
Mountain-like and
Canyon-like
All at the same time.
Surging peaks and troughs
Of a very human kind,
Of a very Earthly kind,
Of a very stellar kind.
Explosions and recreations;
Fertility and vulnerability,

To be born and to die
And to become present in the activity
Of both.
To transmute
The transformation,
Carrying one to another -
Encased by the need and desire
To live in the connectivity
That supports the imaginative nature
Of a joyful life,
With hope and honor
And inquisition.
To move on from where we've been
And where we're going -
Arriving in the exact place we find ourselves.

KANSAS IS A PLACE

Warm evening air,
Winds with humor only soften
By the meeting rivers.
Not quite twilight, but enough to feel reflective,
We traveled along brick buildings and brick roads
Uneven and weathered -
Comforting in their age, complexity and color.
Tender breaths guide the path we walk along.
Kansas is a place of tremoring impulses,
Alive with a dream and dead with despair
simultaneously.
Place of lost culture.
Native blood runs dry.
Babies of new generations
Mending what has been done
And it births itself through murals, through art,
Through music and cigar bars;
Attractive and inspiring.
How lovely that we can transform.
We take more cautious steps now,
And we think about their consequences
A little bit more.
Opening doors instead of closing cavers;
We're working our way into the Earth -
Back again to what is true,
And noble and causatious.

Deeper in honor.
And more connected in feeling.
We become as precious as the architecture,
The pavement,
The bricks,
The land,
The rivers,
And all the fleeting
Creations and observances
That give value,
To our endeavors.

The Painter

Visions surround me
A hurricane of butterflies
Colors melting together
And taking renewed breath
Into uncharted landscapes.
I am new and yet; I am an accumulation
Of everything I've ever been through,
And what I chose not to carry.
I am discernment as well as awe
Simultaneously;
Without compromising the
Character of what I know.
I am released into shades of blue,
Purples, reds and Earth tones.
Unlimited.
I am free -
Without the weight of the past - I let go.
Without the need
Of a thank you,
Or an apology,
Or an explanation.
I am governed
By nobody else's actions
But
My own.

Welcome to the Jungle

How do we keep simplicity
Among a realm of complications?
I have been invited to simplify my life
Many times; but I'm only now truly
Beginning to understand what that means.
The truth of the matter
Is that there are many ways
In which you can choose to live your life.
The how's and the why's are not as important
As the what's.
What is it that you desire to do the most?
And how can you support an environment
That is conducive to it?

Slumber of Solitude

I used to feel my loneliness
Was a burden,
A vast and unshakable discomfort;
Now it fits like a new silk nightgown.
And I wear it in the moments I am suited for
Rest and regeneration.
Slumber of solitude;
It's where I find myself most awake.
Where my greatest ideas
Rightfully assume their place.
And there is a sheen feel
To the impurities
Fear leaves in its wake.
Slipping more confidently
Into my own self-image,
It looks like an excavation;
But I've just hit a valuable material -
And it's still subterranean.
Hidden from passerby
And eyes of those who are preoccupied.
Fatigued by the work required
To bring what's precious
Out into the open;
Though regardless,
I keep going.

The Other Side

If I didn't write,
I don't know where I'd be.
If I didn't dance.
If I didn't sing.
If I didn't attempt to create
Beginnings;
Again and again.
I fear I would have
Confused each wall for a permanent end.
And perhaps that's exactly what they were.
(Or what they seemed)
Time and time again.
The block in the road.
The darkness, the silence, the stillness,
The empty barricade of overwhelming apparitions.
Every fatal end I could imagine;
They all happened before my eyes.
I could feel their occurrences in my skin,
And I was given a white flag
To raise high over my head for submission.
And I felt like surrender was justifiable;
But I came to the conclusion,
That the decision was mine to make.
So I noticed some cracks in the bricks that lay
before me,
Where these walls had always stood.

There was a brightness that was spilling out
And I smelled fresh air pouring in;
So I chipped away, bit by bit,
Until the shadows themselves
Waved their flags of exhaustion
And surrendered quickly with
The weight of the sun.
Turning every ending I've ever known
Into a beautiful transition
I was able to break through.

Daring Ingenuity

Our longings,
Our deepest magnetism,
The discovery of
Our compositions,
Bonded chains of molecular distributions;
We serve and we transport
Our sense of knowing
And we escort what we find
Down highways of enthusiasm.
Encouragement and warnings,
Tricks and pricks and deformities;
We're better off maintaining our openings.
But when we take on water,
It's best to know
When the laceration occurred
And to find its origination;
Quickly.
Instead of pretending
That we're unsinkable.
And taking on too much weight;
More than we can handle.
Because though we may be
Immersed in a world of light and dark;
The physics are inevitable.
And the way it plays out

Can be calculated to the angle.
Only the creative mind
Can come up with something
New.

Only Love

Am I making sense of my past or is
My past making sense of me?
Do we look at each other differently?
Like separated lovers
With different memories?
Trying to sort through
Our discrepancies?
Halfway in moonlight
And readily approaching dawn.
Chasing the orbit
Of who we are;
And who we have become.
Like tails and mice
And other quick and rambunctious things
That are shifting and propelling
Towards me.
Little endurance for shallow waters,
I frequent deep seas of thought.
That's where we dance and rest
And find ourselves once again lost.
And I suppose in an answer
We will always find another question
Until we are left
With only Love.

PERSONAL JESUS

I couldn't reach for you,
Not even if I wanted to.
Hands bound by disbelief,
Twine twisted from fiber
Of distrust,
And braids of sincerity.
I couldn't snap
What I couldn't break through.
Signs of relief,
And progress of relaxation,
There's no use in fighting
What can't be understood.
No game plays
Or criss crosses and arrows
Parading across white boards
Alongside mental preparations.
Because the ultimate truth;
Is that the only one
Who could ever hold you back or
Bind you
Enough to matter;
Is yourself -
And it doesn't take
A genius or a messiah
To figure that out.

Joshua Tree

Blood red scarf
Flickering in the desert sun,
Space to drive
And breathe,
With no one hovering.
No crisis.
No false emergencies.
No sounds louder than the
Muffling winds.
A place where even thoughts
Can have their break.
Unassaulted by vicious expectations
And conforming behavior.
Wear no clothes.
Save yourself.
Get absorbed in the vast nothingness.
Arrive beneath the valiant
Night sky.
Leader of the lost,
Wise poet to the found;
You are the audience.
The star.
The critic.
In this bizarre world,
You are everything;

Go to the places
That make you feel this way.

We're Not Settling

We naturally hit the mark
Of the exact spot that feels good;
When we feel it,
When we acknowledge it,
When we accept it,
When we hold true...
When we arrive at the destination
Of our projected proposals;
Hopefully we are where we inspired to end up.
At least still on the journey and not
Upon the loose brink of forfeit.
Creation is ours to cultivate.
Different forms and different presentations;
Our initiations come from the same place.
Unable to accept less than
What we know
We've been given.

Shapes Of Different Clay

Waiting on promises the years never brought
Fictitious deliveries are always on time,
The truer, are not.
Arrivals and presentations of sore campaigns
We hide behind windows and doors of blame,
Counting minutes like sheep
And shepherding them the same,
We regulate time in pastures
Of our own making.
Green hills and greener still to find,
We never acquit when it's the right time.
Further ahead our gaze appears,
Glassy and fixed –
Like ceramic warriors on the horizon
Frozen in their convicted stances.
Remembrances of the land and footstep forces
Shadows of ancestors cast down before us,
Breathless hunters in an unknown ancient forest.
Stone fallen ruins and hungry winds.
Gravity takes everything back again;
Always to bring it together once more.
Were our best days not as immature atoms?
Space and freedom and fluctuation.
Unrefined people are much less attractive.
And what refines more than tragedy?

More than travesty?
Sculptor in the midst of mastery;
Hands of pain
Moulding curves of new beginnings,
Preparing for the firing
And the reveal of the ultimate outcome;
Different shapes of clay.

To the One Who Mattered

You were my home away from home.
Footsteps I could easily trace
Blindfolded and drenched in moonlight;
You were the last heartbeat
I really had the courtesy
To listen to.
And I recall it's sounds so vividly,
They echo down the halls of my memory.
A comforting feeling, since there's so many
Places that belong to you there.
And it scares me that that's the only place
I can find you now.
Like stumbling upon
A longtime abandoned home -
I too only have courage
To look in from the windows.
You seemed so solid the last time
I saw you,
And I felt like such a disaster.
To dance in between our two worlds;
Is the most honoring heart-ache
I ever knew.
Learning to live with you;
And learning to live without you.

LACK

Alive in times that feel with-drawn,
Scarcity of thought and hopeful willingness.
Misdirected by meddling hands -
Descending from feelings of
Inadequacy and the lack
Of belonging.
But I learned the familiarity
Of this experience from others,
This lack mentality -
And now I'm not quite sure
It is as strange
As is our perspective.
A clear definable quality of our lives;
Metaphysics would tell you they
Are one and the same.
So is it our lack we are magnifying?
Or our refusal to gain?

A Young Man Who Looks Like You

Every young man
Who looks like you
Is a new splinter
In a side of me
I forgot was there.
Benign enough, true.
Innocent enough, yes.
Unplanned; all of it.
I get this unique progression
Our affections took,
But in the deepest part of me
Anyone who looks like you
Has my respect automatically;
Or my complete distrust;
It depends on the day.
Usually my smile
Offers itself a sound familiarity,
A warmth almost shocking
To an unknown stranger.
But, before meeting,
I suppose that was you anyways,
As well as I;
Passing strangers beneath the same sky.
Only touching in present time.
No historical predispositions,

No calculated advances or emotional
Manipulations,
At least, not then -
When I learned your name for the very
First time.
When you smiled
And offered me sunshine
In return,
When you recognized me
Without proof
That I was of value to you,
That I had my shit together,
That I had a college degree,
That I was good in the sheets -
And yet; you saw me,
And acknowledged my value
Without
Weight.
And I relive this moment
Involuntarily
With shy smile,
Each and every time
I see a young man
Who looks like you.

CHERRIES

Bittersweet realities
Night sky and deep breath,
Touches of maroon
With the brightness of peaches.
Flickering sensations
In evening colors,
Melting from one
Back to another.
Day shades of calm appearance
Exposed to the rush of something real,
And joy exists always
In the sharing
Of ourselves.

FAITHFUL AMBITION

Must we wait for the flickering
Flames on a cake?
Must we anticipate a balloon
Flying away?
Must we pick a weed and believe in
The breath that blows
It's seed to the wind?
Must we be beneath a falling star
To glimmer with hope again?
We need not wait for that
Special place.
For that divine time.
For that specific sign.
Each thought is a wish,
Each breath, a prayer;
Each beat the heart emits
Is the presence of a living
Wish.
Life is speaking through us always.
Granting us the power
To manifest the things in which
We believe.
Each moment is a wish unfolding
All we must do,
Is ask.

To Belong

My heart has taken flight
And it knows not
Which direction to explore.
Unbound and loosened from its pulls
Given its own opinion;
It now has to choose.
Wise pauses and calm thoughts
Trusting and hoping it will guide the way.
Slowly shifting from days and days of planning,
Can it function in the moment again?
Oh, so long has passed since it was asked
To make a choice with light influences.
So I wait through days and nights
Of not knowing what's to come,
And I hang to the edge ready to jump -
If I have to.
My thoughts want boats and waves
And something to carry me but I suppose even that
is scary,
For there is no 'safe place' is a storm.
In an elemental upheaval;
There is no place exempt.
No branch unblown,
No river unfilled,
No wave in motion waiting to be stilled -

I guess the movement is healing itself.
Cathartic chaos,
The type that leaves us different;
Somehow changed,
Somehow cleansed,
Rearranged in a way we couldn't have anticipated.
The gloriousness of the moment.
How my body feels when it's in alignment.
But, oh, how it resists an inappropriate obligation.
And, me, left to figure out
What I am really obligated to,
And what my own truth has to do
With what my life looks like,
With what my life feels like,
All the while seeking -
My Ultimate
Destiny.

Our Daily Doses

Tenderizing to the
Point of brutality,
Why is it
Everyone is watching,
But we all turn our heads?
Safest among daisies
And most harmed
Among men,
We fear so much
And anticipate
Ill results.
But our neutral lines
Only expose our inability
To be deeply tolerant.
Locked in a spell,
Obedient to cash flow
And not being rejected
From the pack;
Hunters are killers –
There is no separation.
Blood for blood.
A sharp thirst
And a quick quench.
We take life too seriously
At not taking it seriously

Enough.
Too close to the edge,
Our extinction
Is bound to break.
Concerned with how we're
Perceived,
Compulsively aware of how we're
Performing,
Keeping scores of
Thoughts with no numbers -
We tally unceasingly;
And hesitate accordingly.
Creating ethics and alignments
That may disregard our sanity,
But most environments
Are counter-intuitive anyway,
So we take supplements
But there is no supplement
For playing small.

Sequential

I'm leaping from the cliffs
Of my own creation,
Falling or flying
At a certain point -
You can't really tell the
Difference.
And it doesn't quite matter;
What matters is
How you handle
The ground once you've found it.
How you gain terrain,
And how you move forward.
In different case scenarios of enjoyment,
It's necessary to move
With fluidity,
And not dread.
Disguising our beliefs as
Manageable things,
But frustrated
At the slow results of change.

WHAT HAPPENS IN COSTA RICA

Women meeting
In public spaces,
Gathering and
Holding hands,
Ceremony
And clear intentions.
Cultivations
Of the next steps
Towards healing this
Fragile world.
Hands like stone
And hearts like glass,
We see into each other
Naked and clothed;
Together, but alone.
In ourselves -
Reciting a script
That has yet to
Be written.
Singing songs
That were created
For no other reason
Than to amplify and charge
The great fight;
The fight for ourselves.

To remember our truth;
That the greatest
Master
Lies within our own chest.
With howls
And cleansing dips within fresh waters
We are shedding
The weight of
Unproductive introspections,
With the might
Of the Caribbean waves
We say enough
Is enough,
We are ready to show up
And remain
In the place
Where golden threads
Have sewn our
Hearts together.
Because we know
What weighs on you,
Also weighs on me.
We are stronger united,
So we stand in dedication
Of that.
And however
We choose to live within
Each very different

Fluctuating
Brave and vulnerable moment;
We choose this union.
We will maintain it
First and foremost
For the promise and
Confessions
Between sisters,
Are among the strongest offerings
In becoming accountable
Of our individual
And collective
Choices;
The most powerful
Dynamic
That exists
In our relationship
To one another.

Calm Prerequisites

Far too long you have taken
Poison for water,
Too many days spent
With too high a cost
To be returned,
Too many nights
Crying to the stars
Begging them to come closer
Because you thought
The sun
Would never rise
Again,
Too many worries
When what you needed
Was hope,
But now has come
The moment again
To remember
The perfect cycle
And timing of all things;
For they will happen
Regardless of your hesitations.
My love,
You will blossom again -
I promise.

All that is required,
Is your patience.

UNFURLING UNIFICATION

It won't look how we think.
Mild, quiet, real, lasting.
Stable.
Glowing.
Emanating from the heart.
Retiring the need to be right
(It's wrong)
And instead letting your heart be the guide
(It has been such a long time)
But it's our potential,
It's our destiny,
Our fate that we can't deny, or resist, or
misinterpret.
It's not the time to gawk and mock and poke fun
At the idea that we can live in union,
That we can thrive in harmony,
That we can make a world of a peaceful kind;
It's time to see this as real.
To act on it with your own hands.
To recognize and represent this optimistic
concept.
That's all it is, and that's all it requires.
That is revolutionary action,
To just simply do it differently.
Even if it's one thing,

Let's have the diligence to no longer
Extend our suffering.

CRIMELESS CRIMINALS

It's unfortunate;
My presence wrecked the
Interpretations of your senses.
Annihilating perceptions
Caused on both ends,
Chaotic night parades
Pacing living room carpet,
Pleading for things to be different.
Dark nights turned the living room glow
Into a spot light and nobody knows
Whose really under investigation
Anymore.
Life like a play full of procrastination
And antagonists,
Irritated in our own skin and craving
Our own attention.
We turn the questions towards each other
With twisted eyes and forced smiles,
And we listened and defended
Our positions until bodies went rolling.
Mistrust and deception to ourselves,
By ourselves,
Creating collective disharmony
Because of the discourse within our own cells.
You opened up skies for me,

Insights into the realms of the unforeseen -
A hope in love I didn't have before.
But the paralyzing weight
Of two broken worlds
Contained the wrong
Kind of pressure,
Needed
To mend them.

Lit Fuses

Millimeters of patience
Disengaged or left to revel,
There is a point where it can't
Go any further.
Flights of electric sparks,
We move like spinning tops
Around the perimeter of things
We can't stop to see.
Complex waiting that takes years
To sort through and understand.
Who are we outside of our routines?
We fall between hope and fear.
At times not knowing if we can
Save ourselves,
Or if another will.
So we fire off into the night,
Or become a fluke in the fire light,
But we all come to a point
Where our sizzling
Either fizzles out,
Or burns a whole into the next dimension.

State of the "Art"

Truth doesn't matter anymore,
Ideas change the world.
The affirmations on a passing
Billboard;
Apathy or optimism?
The desert doesn't care.
Positionary stances of
Opposition
WARNING;
Contradictions everywhere.
A world of creative input
But where to lay the first
Stroke,
Where to carve out the first
Crevice,
How do we mold and sculpt
With bound hands and discomforted
Thought?
It's a shame we don't know
Where we left off,
Scrambling for fitting pieces only to be
Left puzzled,
Disheveled;
Demolishers of our own
Construction.

Courageous Emancipation

I'm downset;
I've been up for so long.
I want to be down,
Lay down,
Get down,
Feel the chill in my bones.
Fire has raced for so long
Through my veins from being
So fucking heated from the
State of this place.
It's cool now, from the love
That's been given me.
From the love I've given
Myself.
It's the morphine that helped
My disordered soul.
It's Love that has brought in
Space, and water and
Galaxies of thought.
I remember being caught in
The riptide of fear.
That was before
I saved myself.

Saxophone Highways

Saxophone highways
I want to drive endlessly,
No fog lights or
Street lamps,
Just the ecstasy of the road –
Coming at me full force.
Desecrated gatherings of people;
I wish to be here the most.
Strings of energy
Plucked to a melody
Of familiar songs
Always, somehow, different.
Warm lights and artistic eyes;
This is my jazzercise.
And I like the repetitions.
I find it in every corner of its existence.
On vinyl.
In late night clubs.
And among mystics.
This heart opening feeling
Where the spectrum of humanity
Is seen, shared, and celebrated.
Autonomy naturalistics,
I'm convinced of our attraction
To a positive end result.

Unbiased and uninhibited.
The greatest support;
Could be honesty.
But our convictions are shifty,
And our rationalizations are menacing.
Our greatest freedom is the
Ownership of our feelings.
And rather our greatest support,
May be the willingness,
To let our individual experience
Blossom into a collective one.

As We Sit Around the Astral Table

My dreams have become new
Friends in the night.
They stop by as guests,
And I'm trying to remember
Their names.
Colorful and kind, they invite
Me to contemplate their
Perspectives.
As we sit around
The astral table.
Sipping stardust from
Ancient crystal flutes.
Pouring splits of remembrance,
We celebrate all we've been through.
While simultaneously and
Adamantly summoning possibilities
That are new.
Undreamt,
Unseen,
Storyboarding a bright reality
In which our meetings
May then retire.

Momentous Yearning

I went back to records,
I went back to correcting time tables -
Fractions and divisions
I could mend,
I went back to patience
And cultivating it with things and people
And life events,
Willing to embrace
What I no longer had.
Seeing clearly now,
What was too convenient
To deny
For so long.
So much becoming
And so much distraction to what is true,
No wonder our hearts beat in palpitations -
Excited at too much heartbreak
And the perpetual fear of missing out.
Often misunderstanding the sudden presence
Of a fierceness that may be the onset of a feeling
Right before you do
Something radical.
That intensity of fear
Can often be confused with excitement.
But can we even detect a difference

When we're limited and conditioned
By the lifestyles we've adapted to?
Can we follow our hearts,
If they've been well trained?
And is it fair to require
That the hearts of others
Remain on chains?
I want back may I have this dance.
I want back living room piano playing,
And the dark nights tenderness.
I want to feel again.
And I don't want to do it alone.

TRUE TREASURE

The ampleness of your softness,
The bareness of pink lips with
Nothing to press them against,
The gentleness in the acts
When no witnesses are present.
Tender feelings of unraveled advancements,
Complacency in waiting
For the warm breath deserving
Enough of your affection.
Finding company in books and parks,
Among wise words and tree tops -
Unassuming.
You project to me
The unraveling of a destiny
I never knew could be
So bright and promising.
Foot prints stamped in honesty
And you're jeweled with thoughts
Of the deepest sincerity,
Out of sync with algorithms
You contain a truer feeling
Of what it means to be human,
Bold and encompassing.
You eagerly greet both the beasts and the beauties
And those who have yet to

Disclaim their identification.
As those begin to rise
Who wish to claim none at all.
You are strong.
But only as strong as the rise
Of your last fall.
And you present that openly
In the cadence of your grace,
And the nuance in the shake of your hand.
You feel things.
And you know enough
To know
That wearing your feelings
(Even if they are disagreed)
Is more valuable
Than the most complex
And desired
Diamond ring.

Anarchic Axiom

Poetry;
Lawless territory,
Room for the wild heart,
The heavy heart,
Lines and structures
And boundaries
Caused by both.
Space for all –
Encompassing.
Provoking all truths;
Finding there is really only one.

Unbiased Tenderness

We're people who have learned to ignore each
other.
To avoid eye contact, phone calls and blood-based
Obligations.
To turn away, to shy away, to negate our
disagreements.
To cover-up and deny our own obvious need for
each other.
We walk by and look in every direction but into the
soul;
We look at the floor, the wall, the chair,
Then your skin, your clothes, your hair,
And once we finally
Have arrived at the window of the eyes
The soul seems a little less alert;
A little less bright.
Too in our heads about what we have said to
ourselves,
We become immune to our own dismissive and
aggressive patterns.
Neglectful conditions;
The ones that keep us fixated on our past
And on our own
Judgements.
In the absence of community

What else forms there?
I'll tell you, nothing good.
Congested thoughts; bacteria of the mind,
Parasite to the human kind;
Abandonment.
Dark and crusted condensed disbeliefs
And uncertainty;
Keep us from the openness that we are entitled to
Experience.
The birthright -
To be in the flow of Love while we're living.
True Love;
The Love that can only be shared by the
acknowledgement
That there is sacredness to each breath,
And that the thing required for compassion;
Is unbiased tenderness.

CHERISH

Always aware of itself,
Waking bird in the morning
Singing for no reason at all;
First chirp of the day,
Ceremony to the sun
And celebration of light.
Excited at hellos
And accepting of graceful goodbyes,
Standing alone in the winds sway.
Delicacy of a monarch;
With the endurance of clay,
Granule grades of compacting layers –
Sediment and fossil ridden.
We carry remembrances in every weather,
Fall filled summer dreams,
Always reaching for things we can't touch.
Unsure of where to lay our hands directly
And if they'll be desired
To stay.
In between the ends of touching
And feeling,
There is more to our movement.
Grace fills the space
Left within us
In the wave of decisions.

When Tormented Minds Think Alike

You loop your way inside my mind
So it can be yours to pull upon
At any time.
Sharp turns and swift moves;
Subtlety is not your specialty.
You carve your ways like water,
But with the might of hurricanes
And the temperature of lava.
You feel so justified behind your strings,
Wanting me to be that purity
For all those around me,
But who's the last one to ask how I am doing?
Let alone with the capacity to really understand.
We fluctuate like candles in
A heavy night wind,
Waiting for dawn and some kind of exasperation.
Because each one of us
Has something breathing down our necks,
And our attention is only focused
On how to stay lit.
Digging trenches to preserve
Whatever's left of our wicks,
The deeper we get the harder to see each other.
And we've become accustomed
To this separation.

Just like all roads;
I believe all trenches will lead
To the same hole.
Where our flames will merge
Into a collective bonfire,
And our rage will burn away
In the peace
Of our unsuspecting union.

Unfortunate Happenings and Perfect Departures

The years of my development were soar,
Sore with feeling I am barely now
Beginning to integrate,
Messages and signs and experiences
All knocking at my door -
Whether I was ready for them;
Or not.
Love and misunderstandings;
And Love again.
It seems to be the way of everything.
The more moons I see
And the more sunshine I bask in,
The more it seems to make sense
Of the insensible occurrences.
The ones that brew doubt and charm and courage.
Unfortunate happenings,
And perfect departures.
It all appears right in the end.
The challenge is to stay level headed.
And hopeful.
And clear.
I feel the words I used to scavenge for
To describe my turmoil

Are now melting into a graceful patience;
Which still only comes
After I've felt it all.
And prepare for more of it;
This feeling;
These sensations.
The experience that can't be captured or explained.
No matter how much one meditates or paints,
Or writes,
Or creates.
It's accepting them all,
And remaining open still.
This 'integration' -
Is the greatest art of all.

The Art of Looking Away

For Dr. K

Women
Unearthing toxic ground.
Burials for decaying ethics,
We washed our hands in the river of silence far too
long.
We were warmed in our stillness
By the swelling and crashing
Of stardust and starlight,
Sun struck and fear carved;
Chipping away at the tender pieces -
We were all given a shape
Uncomfortable to fill.
Massive pressures embedded the weight
Of the nightmares and dreams of us all,
Tapping into our well a little bit deeper
Then before,
Finding the source once again.
The attention is now rising,
Resting stories taking their pride
And walking for the first time
Into the global conversation.
With so many 'good intentions'
Why are there so many desecrations to;
The welfare of our people?
The welfare of our women?

The welfare of our children?
The welfare of our men?
The welfare of our elderly?
Faulting the many in need of needing,
Leaving behind those who can't afford
To keep up.
Military mindsets and paper doll desires,
Encampments of propaganda
And the art of looking away -
We shield ourselves from true opinion
Unknowingly.
Delicate female voices lost
In the hurricane of aggressive demands,
What will we have to bear next to release the
burden of
Not being good enough?
Women, the nurturers, the soft ones - why are we
Compacting them into stone?
Brothers, fathers, nephews, architects of the
female heart,
Untrusting encounters of intrusive force
Built walls around us and most people have
fortresses.
Finding our voice is the first chisel
For turning stone to sand.
Women are the water of this world.
The fluid grace, the life-givers, the regenerative
ones;

And yet her choice is often at the end of a man's approval;
Of his taking.
How can a man take something that doesn't belong to him?
As women begin to sing the lyrics of their suffering
Why still the shaming?
Why still the disbelief?
Why still the same ball busting disrespect
Men have always enjoyed when relating with women?
When relating with each other?
When will the arms be extended to hold us?
To nurture us?
To protect us?
To carry us through the release of our pain?
When did the sister, the mother, the lover, the grandmother
Lose its value?
When did women become the poster child for weakness?
When did pussy or bitch become second class citizenship?
Take back your brainwashing tactics and endless semantics;
I'm fine in my own skin.
My scars only tell my stories so my mind
Doesn't have to

File them away
To open them at another time.
Lines of experience paint all of our faces,
Some deeper than others and all that is okay.
Smiles and healthy eyes are
More valuable than pearls.
We must dip into the stickiness of our truth
And use it as honey and molasses,
A thick ingredient to hold things together
And turn out always sweet in the end.
Women;
Honeycombs of teal,
Passion flowers of pink,
And simmering reds of firelight.
We meet in-between the places
Where the world has
Imprinted us.
And it is again we remember,
The body is simply a passport
Collecting stamps of experience,
And ultimately we end up visiting
The ones we favor the most.
Come home -
Back into your seed,
The place before all your blooming.
The power of growth
Is all your own,
It lies within each breath -

Never give away your ability
To harvest your own energy;
To create your own welfare;
To look after yourself;
To speak up for yourself;
To hold the hands of other women,
As we collectively process
Our healing.
As we relearn to sing and dance
And carve with the force
Of a thousand waves,
We take back our place
As masters and tenderers
Of our own hearts.

Benevolent Tanacity

In me I wish you to rest,
May my arms be of use
To hold you in times
Of ferocity,
And entanglement;
As your attachments change
So will your will.
And I encourage you
To trust the leadership
Of your heart.
I desire to nurture you in
Ways that create space for
Your deepest ambitions,
And supports the curious pulse
That has provoked a mind
With more depth than the sea.
I see you.
Do you really see me?
Do we have the capacity to
Love without despair?
Insincerity and dissolution
Have purged lovers of their
True potential.
Dominating quests leave
Scattered dreams bleeding;

I want no such thing.
I simply want that success
Of loving,
Of choosing,
Of sharing.
Tender hearts cower at risks.
We fool ourselves into boastful pride
Of embracing life,
But we tremor at its realness.
I'm impressed by you,
And I know you will do great things,
If you want for yourself
The things I know
You are worth having.

Closing Time

I'm just scared to open up my heart,
Everything is romantic to me.
I could never embrace anything less.
I could never act out of a different place,
Could never occupy a different space.
I broke my own rules.
And I'm glad I did...
Because every moment
Has been beautiful.
I feel I can be disturbed
And still effortlessly
Cheer you on.
A task, a favor - I could be there
In a fragile moment.
I got you covered.
Because, I got you.
I've experienced
From very few people
The effects of being fully invested.
I'm not unavailable
I'm fully prepared;
But meeting you wasn't part of the plan.
And now I've let you in
The front door,
The kitchen and
My bed,
And all though
I have no regrets,
I'm sure you're

Just another romance
I'll have to involuntarily
Forget.

Because You Will Leave

I had dreams of you so sweet.
Wrapped up in a joy that
Is never guaranteed.
We found it in our dance,
In every twist and turn.
We denounced
Our doubt,
And made stronger choices
Deeper in love.
Cocooned in a place only we could see,
Where only we knew we would develop wings.
We took our time.
And navigated remnants of the past;
Gently.
We walked together.
And laid together.
And made love together.
And when I awoke,
I knew that what I had felt
Was best left,
To the innocence and fragility
Of my own conflicted disposition.

Romeo's Retired

Overused balconies,
Stones and outdated structures,
Vines overgrown and the shadow of a space
Granted to only those
Deeply competing in the races.
Stacks of homes like cake layers
It's bound to get tipsy
When our contact is slippery;
And we become top heavy.
Gestures of chivalry
Fall from the hands of men hiding their flaws
And 'good boys' only appear to be lost.
Far beyond the means of responsibility,
Even silence can be anarchy.
We've lost the identity,
Of what feels right
To each of us individually.
So we strive to impress what's in our control,
Hoping acceptance will sneak in like
Mail delivering itself
Straight to the front door.
We act like life will just
Show up for us one day,
Instead of confessing the truth of ourselves
In courageous ways.
The capable seem to be hiding beneath
The decks of their parents place
Praying no one
Will come knocking.

Unknowingly Seeking Union

Steeping from the days activities
Hot water gone cold.
Hard work on the tips of fingers –
There is wisdom found there.
Utterly possessed in a trance-like
Focus.
Sparking interest spins wheels,
Invents things,
Makes things happen.
With no interest, there is no
Attention.
Nothing governing retention.
Sweating out ideas and concepts
Except for those that are the most self-serving,
Purging what we lack the conditioning
To like,
Or appreciate.
Detox the soul of a negative mind.
All arises from calling forth.
Your step, your word,
The gentle pulse of your heart;
All moving in and out of harmony,
Unknowingly seeking union.

CHANGING ALTITUDE

In the spirit of regeneration;
Can we request the adjustments
Of our mindsets?
Is it too painful?
Is it too bashful?
Isn't it too much not to shift?
Pulls and aches and quakes and madness,
Can't we each get to know grace a little differently?
Whose to say how to fly?
It all starts with lifting our wings
And trusting the wind.
Letting go,
So we may ultimately;
Begin again.

How Lovely They Look Dressed in Twilight

People
Will always disappoint you,
They will always fall short
Of your expectations,
Of your needs,
Of the agenda you
Are seeking to be met
By anyone
Other
Than yourself.
Can we not then dream?
Can we not then hold hope
For those we love?
And hang them high between
The sun and the starlight?
So in the evening hours
We can hold reverence
Towards how lovely
They look dressed in twilight,
And the imaginings
Of new and better tomorrows.

Harmonic Concords

Jazz; no need to explain.
Worries, woes gone with
The rain.
Pouring down,
Falling down,
Tickling the sky,
Coming into our own.
Resolving the need
To persevere without pain,
To anticipate without expectation.
To continue when there is conflict.
We all wish that our concerns could be our own.
Our dreams, our nightmares;
Existing just the same,
Explosive in their expression -
Cannot be tamed.
There's not a lot that can keep apart,
Those who wish to unite.
Our brothers keeper,
We can no longer hide the need to
Lift the lid of things that seem
Daunting,
Limited,
Unresolved.
Because we're all sensitive to it.
What does true harmony mean?
It means that we are
Honestly engaged
And truly present.

BLITHE SPURN

I am the most tired.
I am the most broke.
I am the most undefined
I've ever been
And I am the happiest.
I am the most uncertain.
I am the most unexpecting
But I am the most fearless.
Perhaps this struggle,
This perceived possibility of
Impending doom
Is the exact thing
That is teaching me to trust again.
Perhaps by having nothing,
I have nothing left to lose.
Perhaps it is reaching the borderline
Of insanity
To see that it's only what I make of it.
Always is, always will be.
The quality of my work ethic,
The early morning rising,
The struggle of virtue and morality
Doesn't appear as daunting.
Love, companionship -
The only whole.
Everything with a grain of salt,
Learning to manage myself.
It's the warmth from an intelligent lover
That I wish would stay.

So many shiny promises in this place,
Stacks of green and wide eyes easily hypnotized
By scarcity, competition, gain, control, success -
All the misleading bullshit that clogs up your life.
How do we acknowledge that it's wrong but right
Both at the same time?
Well it's neither, so nice try.
Perhaps I got so scared of trying,
Perhaps all the fucks I just cannot give anymore
Have been buried and turned into coal
And now it's all just fucking fuel.
Perhaps I care nothing of what anyone thinks,
Not past, present or future,
(maybe I'm lying)
Or maybe I'm done trying to make the minds of
others
Less heavy than my own
When I'm not equipped for that.
On many levels.
I just want a Love that lets me run around
Naked
And sees the innocence in the mundane,
The life in an infants eyes,
And the universe in a mustard seed.

The Way the Cookie Crumbles

I see men wait at the doorsteps of well-manicured
women.
I see them reach their hands out to women who
are docile and quiet.
I see the women well behaved just enough to catch
a man on a line,
And when comfort sets in
Discards her maturity like
Loose change in her purse.
I see the outspoken women, the expressive women,
The confident and intelligent women;
Standing alone.
Wallflowers at social events.
They intimidate men because they are
Unpredictable,
Uncontrollable;
Masters of inconvenient truths.
I see relationships everywhere courted by young
beauty,
Young thoughts and uninitiated promises.
Forever, they say.
Together, they say.
My heart, they say.
My all, they claim.
But has either the man or woman risen into their
Own power,
Before they decided to use whatever fraction of it
To hold weight and borrow and lend into the
investment of

Another soul?
Playing monopoly with our jobs,
Our dreams and our love life -
No wonder the board goes flying.
Pissed off from corruption and
Articulated buy-outs.
Upgrading to better and better;
When does the seeking end?
When do you finally reach a place
Where happiness sets in?
Is allowed in?
Finds a seat at the table
Next to your spouse and kids.
When did Love become "locking someone in"?
"Doing what's right" - just for the kids"?
We are deceived with our failing expectations.
I was married once,
And there were no fucking rainbows.
So I left never to return,
Until I found someone
Who is wonderfully versed in color.
Who understands their own power,
And desires to learn
More than they
Wish to seek shelter.
Someone
Who understands
Happiness is their own
Responsibility,
And that in accordance
Everything else falls into place.
I, too, had to become what I was looking for.

WRINKLES OF TIME

The road held grooves unknown to me
Landscapes I wish I could take in
As only a passenger has the luxury,
Hurried winds and people and dreams,
So unknowing of their
True potentials.
But they think they do.
Sure, they know -
They have no idea.
Programmed flesh and
Heavy heritage,
How do we smooth out the
Wrinkles of time?
How do we put the iron to
The golden age and recreate
Something new?
What to do when all the children
Have run from the field?
Deserted by our own innocence
How will we remain in tune?
How will we hear the music
Of the stars if we forgot
How to rejoice in silence?
Shallow hills make moles of us all.
Neglected valleys grow dry
As we burry ourselves beneath the earth.
Dormant wisdom of who we were
I feel the shame, but I long
For peace more.

When You've had Enough

If the truth no longer matters,
If there is question of ones
Cause,
If there is reason to believe
We should hesitate at all,
Let us have the courage to
Answer our calling.
Grant us the strength and the
Forthright momentum, the honest presentation,
And an uninhibited proclamation.
No longer can we seek the advice
And council of others.
Convoluted seas of poisoned opinions,
Shipwrecked without a compass.
Sails with too much wind.
We ask others to fix our brokenness;
Use your magic, your tongue,
Use your source and heal my wounds.
But of coarse no one else's touch
Carries more power
Than your deeply seeded beliefs.
It's not why or how we get ill,
It's how do we get better.
It's not the problems
That require so much attention,
It's the answers.
Does it mean we need to know?
No, but it means we must hone in
On our solutions.

We must boldly carry
Patience for ourselves,
For others as well,
For the world.
Inventing new ways to be better
Rather than condemning dysfunctional behavioral
patterns.
Old paradigms.
They're failing.
We think we're failing ourselves,
But we're not.
If 'they' robbed us of anything,
It is our ability to dream.
Our ability to trust ourselves,
To trust the competency of others,
To know our own power, to know our value.
To see the world as a safe and comforting place
Instead of reckless and unsupportive.
We're among a great revolution
That is yet to be realized,
That is yet to be televised,
And it will not come
When you are comfortable.
It will come
When you've finally had enough.

Because There is No Channel or App

I felt my feet pressing
Upon the grass.
Shallow indentations temporarily
Forming the trace of my steps,
Heavy and full of flickering emotion.
A days work worn like
Wool in summer,
Feelings like fish deep in my belly,
Waiting in a daze in the soft pink light
Of the evening sun.
The geese had already flown home
And it was the quiet build of night,
Where everything is still
But the bats and first set of stars,
The sky yawns and blinks it's tired eyes
Into deep purples
And I'm eager to watch the galaxy awake.

Gender Avatars

Words linger in my head
Spoken from every man I have ever known
So cute,
So wet,
So tight,
So admirable,
So beautiful;
As if my life and heart beat
We're governed
By their courageous
And loose
Observances.
Their dear confessions,
Their enthusiastic agreements -
As if my existence
Was somehow now more
Valid.
Or my birthright
Outside of being objectified was
Finally initiated
And somehow; now,
I'm more real.
The truth is I was whole
Before I entered the eye line
Of their misled
And bold
Approvals.
As if before their
Revolutionary discovery

I didn't have the capacity
To exist on my own,
And in my own right.
Within the sanctity
Of myself;
Within the fulfillment
Of my own being.
But - this is the exact place
I have been
All along.
My shelter and my home;
Where I will remain
Long after you are gone.
So ask me,
How is it that you respect a woman?
And do you see something liberated or
Contained and limited by your own desires and
self-interest?
And how quickly you move into her terrain
As if it is your own.
Acknowledging her qualities;
Her smile,
Her curves,
Her softeners,
Her warmth,
But these things
We're not put on this earth
For your comfort -
They are for hers.
Every atom
Every nuance of feeling,
All her own.

Organically occurring in her own flesh,
Fully alive solely for her own benefit.
You just happen to be passing by.
So you would be wise
To lay down the programmed impulse
For the love of a woman to be
As a crusade.
Whether it be her body,
Or her heart,
Or her soul.
Instead of saying too much too soon
Shooting blank compliments and empty promises
Just to get her in the bedroom —
Try meeting her in a space
That is free from
Conquer,
Competition,
And the denial of one's own wounds.
The ones so easily projected and expected
To be taken care of.
For this is not her duty.
You're inability to love,
Even fleetingly,
Will show itself in the way you touch her skin.
Whether it comes from compassion and the
Interest of her own needs,
Or only through the eyes of your own.
She must be loved
Wildly,
For being wild
Is her true nature.
She must be held as the centerpiece

Of your passionate behavior,
For she holds the key through her pleasure
To many secrets you do not yet know.
She must not be limited
By a concept,
A category,
An idea,
Or an expectation.
Because her freedom and it's celebration,
Her freedom and it's attainment,
Her freedom and it's security,
Is undoubtably linked
With the emancipation
And initiation
Of your own.

Ingress Cognizance

Maybe I was feeling heavy
Because the rain was on it's way,
Maybe I thought the tears
Were my own.
I'm healing myself of a defeated
Mentality.
The rain isn't just tears,
It's cleansing; a regenerative phenomena.
Elixir to flowers,
And birds,
And people.
The light nature of it's
Quietness,
The giving back of it's birth,
The endless falling
From sky to earth,
The nourishment -
The celebration.
Every molecular exchange
In flow,
In water,
In rain.
Containing in everything,
And in everything - contain.
Mirror, life force;
Holder of the collective mind,
Will always make new life
When exposed to sunshine.

Surefire Precepts

Real time desires
How to attain them
When time is forgotten?
Our soft haven of comforts
Belated by our need to rush.
Excited; we're discovering
Less and less of things
Containing true value.
Astounding how we decipher
What is important,
How we measure the success
Of our endeavors -
The mirror to check
To make sure
We're doing it
Right.
Despite what we know to be true;
We play the fool
And convince ourselves
That we're nothing more
Than the scraps of shiny things
We've diligently sewn together.

From Wine to Water

I missed the smell of you.
That was unknown to me
Until we got close enough
For our cheeks to brush.
As our embrace became the only thing
I was thinking about,
A single minded focus on how good
The entrance into your arms was;
And the place I like to be,
The warm place where our two bodies meet,
Where I'm not thinking -
Isn't this what they call meditating?
I don't know but I speak your name
As a new mantra inside my brain -
Effortless.
That's what it always felt like.
But the dark places we like to hide
Complicated everything.
Our belief could never have been in each other;
If it was never our own to begin with.
Absent from our own independent validations
An acclaimed name that was blessed,
And wasn't yet cursed by our own tongues.
How can Love be this thing
That we first have to create
In order to feel?
In ourselves
First building kingdoms that can endure,
Weather and famine,

Hardships and war;
Is it not then that we are fully competent to unite?
That we then come to see eye to eye?
That the fight
Is never between the other?
We instead become an encouraging presence
While also ironically
Simultaneously
Alongside in battle.
And why, then, to believe and to trust
Appears to be an errand
We don't seem to wish to run?
Why is the responsibility to understand each other
So negotiable?
And why does it show itself as defense?
And why do we have so many mechanisms of
hatred?
And so few but commonly mocked and criticized
attempts at peace?
What are we really offering each other?
Because now would be a great time
To move from wine to water.

New Virtues

Headed towards our most desired destinations
Whether they be literal or metaphorical,
They are real none-the-less.
Places and feelings all our own
Why is it we should deny ourselves the truth
Of what we really want to do?
Shouldn't it be as available
As the aspects of ourselves
That we hold dear?
We shouldn't covet
Any part of who we are,
So why would we try?
Give up and get down -
It's time to make
New virtues.

Compulsive Blunders

Fucks I could have given,
Volunteering in the form of tolerance;
I'm no longer interested in making things
Clean,
Unless it's my own
Kitchen floor.
Endless chaos
In the form of endless disasters.
Self-created hurricanes and earthquakes of
Emotion
That bring total annihilation to the structure
Of whatever the person was
Before the occurrence.
Damage happens.
And it happens naturally.
So why rush the process?
Why start fires
Just because the brush
Is dry?
Why come untied
At any moment
That is inviting you to?

When You Fall

Come to me;
My child,
My love,
My eternity.
Bathe in the river
And bask in the
Forgiveness
Of the stones;
Purify and
Let go,
Show us what
Tears you have let
Gone dry,
Release
Whatever
You need to,
So that you may
Rise
To become
Mightier
Than the weight
Of the mountains.

The Old Hotel

My feet feathered on treaded carpet,
Wallpaper intricacies touched by souls
A million times before,
Somehow still fresh with new hopes
And the guarantee
That new eyes will smile
And form tears where they have
Always been shed.
Haunted hallways create union with new memories
And we are taken back to a time
Much more simple,
Yet hidden within the same complexities.
How are we to know if we are moving forward
Or moving backwards anyways?
Lines and confessions only go as far
As we're willing to admit.
So we hold each other in moments of doubt.
We aim to create the best of what we have
And leave the rest up to a name too precious to
utter.
We navigate patterns
Of those preserved places
That our energy
Is attempting
To be remembered,
But we are always left
With nothing more
Than the experience
Itself.

Own It

Epileptic convictions
Prescription drugs abound,
And no one's got any damn sage.
Blind leading the blinder,
Yet we gawk at those leading
Their own way.
Though secretly, we are wishing to do the same.
We may not throw rotten tomatoes anymore,
But our opinions are the same fucking thing.
And the irony is; it's even more messy.
We loose our trust within our aggressions
For another and eventually; for ourselves.
My sustainability has become decay.
And my decaying is my revolution.
So what is right or wrong with that?
Except what's collectively agreed upon.
Parental eyes everywhere
But I thought I only had two,
Or three,
Or maybe four true guardians.
Our lives are far outside of our jurisdictions.
And yet; solely our own.
Unfoldments and endangerments,
Ceremony and celebrations,
It can't all fit neatly into
An essay,
Or bank statement,
Or a conversation.
More often than not I find myself

Come into alignment
Only to receive the force of 20 quarterbacks
Hidden all the while from my view.
Dressed as teachers and neighbors
And people I thought I knew better.
But who really knows who anymore?
These days or any day for that matter?
And isn't that a mystery?
But also, kind of epically exciting?
To know you are the one representative,
The only politician,
The sole leader and religious practitioner;
For nothing but
Your own soul.

When a Double Negative Becomes a Positive

Hands of friends,
Loose grips and sweaty palms;
Am I trying to be held
Or am I just losing touch?
Drifting away from what I don't identify with,
It's causing me to return to corners
I'd rather run from.
Erratic stairs and usual beggars of forgiveness;
No one is begging at my door.
No requests to stay or forgive,
Or love again;
Just
Abandonment.
And hey, by now -
I'm used to it.
I don't believe the world is as sad
As it is alluded to seem,
It's just the heavy reality of departing;
The shock of disappearance,
The scream that reminds you of your aloneness.
The siren of absence
Is ironically the inviter
Into your own soul.
It's this leaving that tears us apart.
It's the story we spin of how and why it happened.
How we ignored signals or could have
Been more bold in our responses.
Or how we are faulted in some way
That made it impossible for the other to stay.

Our explanations can be vile.
The devil is always alive in the details
And a story is always that; influential.
Word of mouth,
The game of telephone between our
Head and our heart can be convoluting.
Something's bound to get lost
When we get too critical.
Chances for redemption linger in our own
acceptance,
Better beliefs often can come out of this loss.
Self-love is a radical thing and it may irritate
Any pre-existing programming;
(Including but not limited to)
Insecurity, anger, resentment,
Jealousy, blame and vanity.
It can trigger a deep re-evaluation forcing us to
Retire personality defining characteristics
And retire habitual practices that dominated
Who we thought we were.
So we can become who we're meant to be.
So that we don't have to feel alone anymore,
In the presence
Of our own company.

Harmonic Feats

The shadows in the moonlight,
The tenderness found in the winds breeze,
Tempting souls of all kinds to come out and play.
We sort through darkness
Like avid treasure hunters
Finding pieces of starlight,
Diamond, gold and sapphire.

Paths unfold in a wooden field,
Grave arrangements canceled in potent silence
Of something larger than the trees.
Keeping company
To dwellers of the night
And holders of the evening sun.

When the war runs out
And the honors are served,
We wear the badges
Coated with the hope of a future
Without the polarities
That come
From misunderstandings.

ALMOST 30

I'm dreaming of you almost every night.
Sounds fade and rise again,
And I am dormant.
Letting go is a craft I assumed perfected by now,
So why is it your memory is still so active and alive?
Time has transitioned
And so have I,
But you'll still find me
In the same coordinates.
So often I must convince myself
That I do not have
The luxury to hallucinate
And perceive things as unchanged,
When even the color of my eyes
Contains a different and unfamiliar
Glint.
I still have that floor model couch,
But I do not care anymore
If the dogs get on it,
Or paint,
Or spaghetti sauce.
Vacuuming has proved useless, but I still do it.
I call spiders my friends now
Instead of chasing them out
Because there are just too many.
There are corners my fingers haven't touched
Since the last time they touched you,
And I've learned to take things
Radically less serious

Then I used to.
And who knows if I would pass the test
For the qualification
Of domesticated house wife's best
But I have a lot of heart,
And enthusiastically put effort into
Communication and creative solutions.
And while my attention to dust
Seems to have waned,
My power is fierce
And my self-respect has become
Fully regained.

CRAZINESS IS LIKE HEAVEN

When I feel things the most deep
Is when I feel the most alive,
Is when I feel the most excited,
Is when I feel the most frightened,
Is when I feel things are the most at stake;
When the world is rising and falling
In the same breath,
When the tenderness becomes rock
And rock becomes tenderness,
And we are given reason to let go –
And hold on,
In the same thought.
And we have this sensation
That neither is truly possible.
Because in union – there is no grasp or release;
It's about learning to immerse yourself in the
Connecting singularity.
To feel a sensation without the lust of possession.
Without the desire for agenda.
Without the need to occupy anything other than
The space of the unknown.
This is the land of the living,
The land of insanity,
Even Jimi Hendrix said 'craziness is like heaven'
And he wasn't kidding.
People walk paths of numbness
And convince themselves it's a natural
Or even desirable
State.

That feeling itself is a luxury, or for tree hugging
hippies,
Or for old people, or children, or women,
Or people who aren't strong.
But the fact of the matter is,
Is that feeling requires extreme bravery,
And bravery meets you higher on the mountain
Than strength;
It has more endurance.
And it has more say so when in conversation
With your success.
Feeling gives more life to your breath,
And more breath to your life,
And it's intended to
Build you up and navigate you like the stars,
So don't judge
The shapes of
Your own constellations.

GOWER ST. BRIDGE

So many things in life have no guarantees,
No promises;
No immediate relief.
It's easier to fall behind,
And harder to get ahead.
Cyclical systems tripping us up,
Being alive as a human being isn't as complicated
As greed has made it out to be.
Still we strive, and dream, and struggle.
Still we believe, and hope, and encourage.
Still we fall, and cry, and sing.
Expressing in the only way we know how to;
With the magnitude of our entire soul.

More Than an Economic Recession

If I must hear another undeserving confession,
Another warrior surrendering
Minutes before finishing a
Vision,
If I must hear of another mission paralyzed by
indecision;
I may come undone.
And it's clear somehow
That this sense of lack or stagnation
Must hold weight in my own life -
Right?
Are we what we perceive?
Many would tell you; of coarse we are.
Is it continually the wrong relationship?
Or is it a warp in the way I approach myself?
Many would say there is no difference.
I'm often consumed in my own questions,
And they test the flexibility and elasticity of this
world.
I see happy people in shamed places
And shamed people right where they're supposed
to be.
Is this actuality or our true reality?
Or are we continually affirming ourselves?
Regardless of what is right.
And once again;
In there lies
No difference.

Drink Less, Dream More

Exasperated endeavors,
Depleted accounts,
And casualties of misplaying -
It's so interesting
How the unfoldment of our lives
Comes at the complete annihilation
Of our projected plans.
We fall apart and trip on the pieces
Of ourselves that were always intended
To be shed,
The desecration is in our disappointment
With our potential before it's even
Had time to take form,
Omnipresent fermented toxicity,
Flooding dreams of fools
And invading the days of optimistic minds;
Until the definition of dreaming has become
Redefined.

Human Cookies

Hallucinations of life in the form
Of shocking imagery
And retiring belief systems,
Phantom postures of a world phasing out
Which ones are ghosts
And which ones are apparitions?
Which ones are from the past
And which ones are from the
Future?
Can we all see the same things?
Or is it the projections of a spectrum
Of different beliefs?
I think I've found the place that is
Untouchable within me -
And it's really exciting.
The place where the force of life seems equivalent.
Buoyancy of the soul
I've learned to
Push through the limits of who I was trying to be.
I don't intend to have a lifetime
Of recreating the same day
Over and over again.
I've realized I don't have to fit in, but
I do have to do something about it and
Take responsibility for my own shit.
Following adorned signs but knowing nothing
about signals,
We must choose where we wish to turn.
Always, this turning;

The choices never cease,
They just become more in alignment
And move with better
Ease.
I fall into meditation these days
The same way I fell into
Anxiety.
The madness can only reach such an intensity
Until that, too, slows its heart beat.
Fortunate gatherings of like minds,
Rare, like scientists discovering a new species.
Now moving into new territory;
And we can see why it can be perceived as a
struggle.
Wide eyed and forgotten
We're rising into ourselves
Quite nicely.
I used to be armed with a lot of resistance,
An arsenal of what I knew I was
And wasn't capable of;
But now I do not know.
Things I thought I'd do have not come,
And the things I anticipated would be impossible -
I have accomplished.
So I'm entering a different place
Where I don't have to
Know everything.
And everything is somehow possible.
I'm no longer limited to the shape on the tray
That was cut for me
When I was born.

Spontaneous Conditions

Carefully articulated desires,
Impulses build up one at a time.
After all we are what we
Approve or deny ourselves to.
How are we so good at punishment?
When it is such an inorganic act?
How conflicting to our natural
Talent of creation.
Our judgements are nothing but
Destructive.
No matter how many hours
We spend litigating validation
For our views
And mindsets
And stipulations -
Even the things we praise
Are in service of our conflicts.
Drama; it's not about creating it,
It's not about avoiding it,
It's not about defining it.
It's neutralizing the reality
That we can't always predict
What happens next.

I'm Ready to Be In Love

Four arms caress warm flesh,
Tangled hair and heavy breath;
I want you,
I need you,
I must let you go.
Phasing in and out of
The ebb and flow,
Soft lips
And eyes that forgive,
Are we always emotionally
Living out of a backpack?
When do we decide to officially
Move in?
You increase my heart rate
But do you really want to know
What makes it beat?
Fertile grounds for the cultivation of things,
Simple as well as great in complexity
How do I only show you a part of me?
Hands down, you're gonna see the whole thing.
I'm not a puzzle, you will not have to assemble me,
I'm more like a flower
I like crisp air and room to breath.
Life has entrusted me the company
Of many who seem to pass through,
Honored and disturbed differently
By how someone
Chooses to show up.
I'm so sick of being the greeter,

Or the damage control,
I'm ready to be in love -
And take control of my story
Without a deep narrative of how it should end.
I'm supporting the impulse
To live in rhythm with the sun,
And in harmony with my surroundings -
I'm tired of pretending
We're broken glass
That won't piece back together again.
We are earth and mud
And softer than we let on,
Malleable as dough
We rise just the same,
And we dance in the places
We find the most freeing.

RECONDITE ADORATIONS

Dizzying sleep,
Restless perplexity and
Heightened curiosity -
Trust stretched thin.
Reaching in the direction
Of you; too sure to be confused.
Too vague to be settled.
Excited still,
In spite of so many unknowns.
But to carry on -
To continue on,
We must agree
In the mutual value
We acknowledge
In the dreams,
Existing independently
Within
Each others
Hearts.

Doing and the Not

The glint of the morning sun brought the invitation
Of a new day.
The heavy memory of twisted dreams made
The waking up hard, heavy - but necessary.
Allegiance to visions
And things of a productive kind.
I don't need a 'happy' life.
But a purposeful one.
Renewing my adventuring.
Renavigating the call of my heart.
Telling myself indeed I am the only person
Who needs to see me.
I am the only project that
Needs fixing.
I am my own focus and goal and progression.
Why do we always take on outside tasks
Without ourselves first being complete?
Fascinating, isn't it?
The grace of hands that put things into order.
How very compelled we become at another's pain
or impatience.
The point is there is no damnation.
No irrevocable action.
There is the doing and the not.
There is nothing else.

Effortless Embrace

It took a while
For my memories
To call forth the courage
To represent themselves;
For my details to become a thing
Of analyzation
Let alone;
Celebration.
Things take time
That are worth reestablishing,
And all your stories
Deserve a little editing,
And in light of our effectiveness
And retelling our experiences,
Perhaps, naturally, we make sense of
Our suffering.
In ways that suit us individually.
I used to dress myself up
In many different ways,
Literally and - metaphorically.
But I have now come
More truly to understand
To love how
I can rearrange
Myself
Without even trying.

Made in the USA
Middletown, DE
16 November 2022

14915146R00110